Desert Night
Desert Day

by Anthony D. Fredericks
illustrated by Kenneth J. Spengler

Books for Children

Bristly hair,
    Tusks—beware!
Javelinas
    Eat prickly pear.

Stingers lash,
   Whip, and dash.
Scorpions grab
   In a flash!

Nuzzling nose—
Sleep and doze.
Young fox rests—
Quickly grows.

Leaping, popping,
    Seldom stopping.
Tiny rats—
    Hip, hop, hopping!

With voices strong,
A concert long.
Coyotes sing
Their lonesome song.

Now night is done.
New day's begun.
Daytime critters
Greet the sun.

A heated breeze
    Through mesquite trees.
Lizards be-bop
    In twos and threes.

Dash, rush, scurry,
Sudden flurry—
Running rabbits
In a hurry!

Slipping, sliding,
Watching, gliding—
Banded kingsnake
Darting, hiding.

Landscape sweeping,
Old beast peeping—
Desert tortoise,
Slowly creeping.

Regal head,
    Tails of red—
Hawks are soaring
    Overhead.

Through the day,
In jeweled array,
Butterflies
Dance and play.

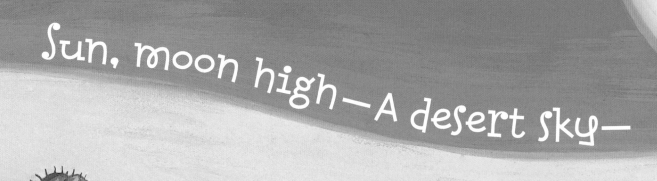

Sun, moon high—A desert sky—

Busy creatures crawl, run, fly!

The desert is home to a wide variety of animals. Some are nocturnal (nock-tur-nal). They sleep during the day when it is hot and are awake at night. That's why you seldom see them. Other desert critters are diurnal (die-ur-nal). Like you, they are awake during the day and sleep at night. When they are awake, they hunt for food or may hide from their enemies.

The Sonoran Desert stretches across southwestern Arizona, southeastern California, and parts of northern Mexico. In summer, temperatures are hot—REALLY HOT! Sometimes it's over 120 degrees in the day. At night, temperatures may drop to a "cool" 70 degrees. Sonoran Desert animals have adapted to this wild and wonderful place.

Nocturnal Animals
[NIGHT TIME]

ELF OWL—Elf owls live in the abandoned nests of Gila woodpeckers. These nests are dug into the side of a saguaro cactus. Elf owls are tiny birds with rounded heads, yellow eyes, and a greenish-yellow bill. Tiny, squeaky babies stay in the nest until they are one month old. They like to eat insects and other small animals.

JAVELINA—The javelina is the only wild, pig-like animal found in the United States. Although they look similar to pigs, javelinas are much smaller. They are most active in the evening and enjoy eating prickly pears because of the high water content. Javelinas have good hearing, but very poor eyesight.

SCORPION—Scorpions rely on their sense of touch to locate prey. Often, a scorpion walks around with its claws spread apart until it bumps into a spider or insect. Then, it grabs it! Sometimes it uses its stinger. A scorpion's stinger is a hollow tube connected to a poison gland near the end of its tail.

KIT FOX—Kit foxes live throughout the deserts of North America. A mother will nurse her four or five babies while the father hunts for food. Kit fox families stay together until the young are ready to live on their own.

KANGAROO RAT—Kangaroo rats only weigh between 1 and 6 ounces. They hop over the ground just like a kangaroo. Their hind feet are large with hairy soles that aid in jumping in loose, soft sand. They live in underground burrows and eat seeds gathered during the night.

COYOTE—Coyotes sometimes come out during the day and at twilight, but are most often seen (and heard) during the night. About the size of a medium-size dog, these familiar desert creatures make howling, yelping, or barking sounds that can be heard for long distances. They usually live in dens and come out to hunt for both plants and small animals.

Diurnal Animals
[DAY TIME]

SIDE-BLOTCHED LIZARD—This multicolored lizard is always out during the summertime, even when the temperature is over 100 degrees! They can be found sunning themselves on boulders. They are usually light brown in color and may have light blue bands along the tail. They like to eat insects, and can grow up to 15 inches long.

COTTONTAIL RABBIT—These animals are often out in the early morning hours or late afternoons. Usually they spend their waking hours eating grass or the leaves from short plants. Their light brown color and short tails help them hide in the rocks where they live. When running, they can reach speeds of 20 mph—zigging and zagging through the desert.

COMMON KINGSNAKE—The common kingsnake is a nonvenomous snake—it does not have any poison. It gets its name because it often eats other snakes, including rattlesnakes. It also feeds on lizards, small mammals, and eggs. Sometimes, when attacked, it will roll into a ball.

DESERT TORTOISE—These slow-moving, prehistoric-looking creatures may live to be well over 100 years old. Their shells grow to lengths of nearly 15 inches. They like to crawl into burrows to escape the desert heat, but will sometimes come out to look for plants to eat. A desert tortoise is able to live where the ground temperature reaches 140 degrees.

RED-TAILED HAWK—The red-tailed hawk weighs between two and four pounds. Females are larger than males, with a wingspan up to 56 inches. A red-tail will soar high overhead giving a hoarse scream, and using its sharp eyesight to locate small animals on the ground. Most of its diet consists of rodents; although it will also eat snakes and lizards.

PAINTED LADY BUTTERFLY—This insect is found throughout the Sonoran Desert. It is light orange in color with white spots and black edges on its wings. Before it can fly, it must warm up in the morning sun. Then, it dances through the desert looking for flowers, especially lupines. It sips the nectar from these flowers throughout the day.